Native Americans
Customs, Costumes, Legends, and Lore

Written and Illustrated
by Gina Capaldi

Good Apple

Deepest gratitude to my father, son, mother, H.S., and entire family. Special thanks to my editors, Suzanne Moyers and Susan Eddy, for their enthusiasm for this project.

Senior Editor: Susan Eddy
Editor: Suzanne Moyers

GOOD APPLE
An Imprint of Modern Curriculum
A Division of Frank Schaffer Publications, Inc.
23740 Hawthorne Boulevard
Torrance, CA 90505-5927

ISBN 1-56417-668-1

   3 4 5 6 7 8 9 PAT 01 00 99 98

Contents

Introduction

Although there are more than two million Native Americans living in this country today, they are not the dominant culture they were before the arrival of European immigrants. So why learn about them? Why the fascination with a history so different from "our own," and one whose voices reach us mostly from the dusty archives of archaeology?

The fact is, Native American history is *our* history, from the well-known story of how Massachusett Indians helped the Pilgrims survive to the models of democracy loaned to us by the Cherokee and Iroquois. Native Americans and later Americans are bound together in a common, and often harrowing, story of both triumph and loss.

In this book, children will discover how the ideals, beliefs, and geographic surroundings of various Native American tribes shaped their everyday customs. Hands-on individual and group projects are intended to expand students' understanding of each culture at a more insightful level than might be experienced from a purely textbook-based approach.

The activities in *Native Americans: Customs, Costumes, Legends, and Lore* are intended to inspire a *historical* understanding of each tribe. Because the spiritual beliefs of Native Americans really can't be separated from their everyday customs, ceremonies and rituals become an important vehicle for exploring that history. We've tried to approach these issues with an attitude of respect and with the intention of communicating both the mystery and complexity of Native American traditions. We hope you'll do the same.

Suggestions for Using This Book

You can use the information and projects in this book as the main component of your Native American curriculum or to supplement textbooks and materials you already use. The stories and projects provide practice in language arts, critical thinking, cooperative learning, math, and social studies skills.

In each chapter you'll find

- background information detailing the history, customs, and traditions of a specific group of Native Americans
- a retelling of a tribal legend
- reproducibles showing a traditional woman and man from each tribe, everyday tribal tools, and dwellings that students can decorate by following the color code provided. Use these pages as coloring sheets or in one of the projects described on pages 7-8.
- step-by-step directions for group and individual projects based on Native American culture and history

You also get

- a bibliography listing extra resources for you and your students, including literature, professional books, and software

- a colorful map poster showing Native American men and women of various regions dressed in traditional costumes, along with the special tools they used every day

How to Use This Book

Start by sharing background information with children. Show them the figures for each tribe and discuss clothing styles and how they reflect the traditional roles of different people in the tribe, as well as the tribe's history and mythology. Look at the everyday artifacts and help children connect the way objects look with their practical uses.

Next, distribute copies of the reproducibles to children. Share some of the following ideas for using the elements on the reproducibles, but also encourage student suggestions.

Basic Materials

- corrugated cardboard, foam board, or clean meatpacking trays
- posterboard or oak tag
- scissors
- tempera paints
- white glue
- silicone glue
- hole punch
- thread or string

Dioramas

1. Enlarge dwelling using a copy machine. Paint.

2. Trace dwelling onto posterboard and cut out, leaving a 1-inch (2.5 cm) flap at the bottom so it will stand upright. (Figure 1)

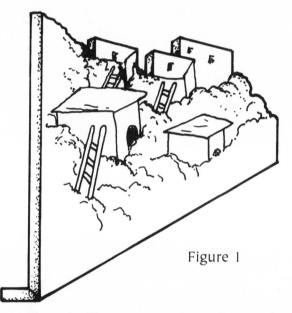

Figure 1

3. Mount dwelling on template; glue in place.

4. Repeat process with the tools and costumed figures.

5. Glue or tape figures into shoebox.

Other Tips:

- Use natural materials, such as leafy twigs for trees, in your dioramas. These materials can also help you camouflage the tabs on the figures and artifacts.

- Place samples of real or papier-mâché tribal foods next to individual dioramas. For example, clay pots filled with Indian corn might be positioned near a diorama depicting the Southwest Indians.

- Use cardboard larger than the diorama to add painted backdrops of forest, mountain, or desert scenes. Glue these scenes behind each diorama.

Three-dimensional Posters

1. Make posters detailing the geographic surroundings of Indian groups.

2. Enlarge dwellings, tools, and figures. Cut out and paint.

3. Trace enlarged shapes onto foam meatpacking trays or corrugated cardboard and cut out.

4. Mount figures and other objects onto foam cut-outs.

5. Attach objects to posters using silicone glue. (Figure 2)

(Note: The thicker the foam or cardboard, the more three-dimensional your posters will appear.)

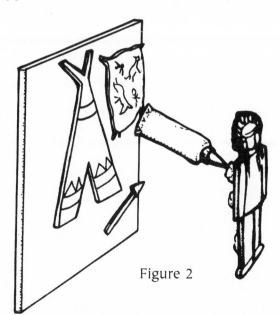

Figure 2

Mobiles

1. Enlarge and cut out dwellings, then mount on lightweight posterboard.

2. Copy, cut out, and mount figures onto separate posterboard. Overlap figures onto dwellings and glue in place. (Figure 3)

3. Punch small holes at even intervals along the bottom edges of dwellings.

4. Mount tools onto posterboard. Cut out. Punch holes along the top edges of each tool.

5. Thread tools with lightweight string, thread, or fishing line. Tie onto dwellings so that they hang freely. (Figure 4)

Figure 3

Puppets

1. Mount figures onto oak tag or cardboard. Cut out.

2. Add craft sticks for holding puppets.

3. Embellish props, costumes, and backdrops with tribal symbols shown in this book.

4. Write scripts from legends included in this book. Make additional characters to represent other characters in the scripts.

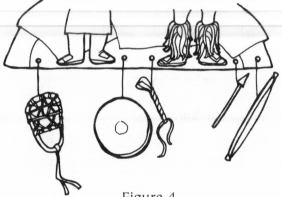

Figure 4

Native Americans of the Far North

Background Information

The land of the Far North Indians includes all of Canada, the northern part of the Great Plains, and the rim of the Arctic Circle.

There were hundreds of scattered tribes roaming this area at one time. The larger groups were the **Chippewa (Ojibwa), Cree, Micmac, Carrier, Ingalik,** and **Dogrib.**

How They Survived

Summers in this area brought heavy rains. Winters brought snow and extreme cold. The Far North Indians invented many ways to live in this challenging environment. They learned to move over the snow by using toboggans, or sleds, and snowshoes. The most common form of dwelling was the wigwam. The Indians who lived on the frozen tundra covered their wigwams with animal hides.

Clan groups were isolated from each other for weeks or months at a time. Children were raised to be independent and respectful of one another's freedom. Some people believe that this sense of respect explains why wars were very unusual among Far North Indians.

Everyday Customs and Beliefs

The Chippewa tribe elected individual leaders for each village. The leader was responsible for all decisions that would affect the group. Though groups of Chippewa lived far apart, they still considered themselves part of one big family. Clans, or groups of related families, had names like Crane, Fish, Loon, Martin, Deer, and Bird. Each clan had a special responsibility or job in each tribe. For example, members born into the Fish clan had the job of helping to solve disagreements among other clans.

Fishing
Decoy

FACT

Chippewa boys smeared bear grease on their hair before braiding it.

FACT

Because a bear standing on its hind legs looks like a man, the Cree Indians believed that bears understood human language.

The Far North Indians believed that every power in nature had a spirit. When they saw the Aurora Borealis, or Northern Lights, these Indians believed the spirits were dancing and having a good time. The winds were considered to be four brothers. The greatest wind came from the north to punish evil people. The brother from the west wind was known as being generous and offering good hunting. The east wind brother was stingy and offered the Indians little food. The wind brother in the south provided foods such as berries and roots.

Europeans Bring Change

European fur traders made their way into the Far North around 1670. Traders taught the Indians how to use a new machine called a steel trap. The trap did most of the hunter's work. Trading companies, like the Hudson Bay Trading Post, encouraged Indians to hunt as many animals as they could to make money, but many Native Americans considered the traps cruel because they often caused the animals to suffer before they died.

A flu epidemic killed many Far North Indians. As more animals were killed for their fur, the Indians began to starve. They were forced to move into the territories of other Indians. Wars broke out.

Chippewa Purse

FACT

A favorite food of Indians living in the cold Far North was beaver meat, which is full of fat and provides long-lasting energy.

Carrier Snow Walker

The Story of the First Earth (Chippewa)

The creator of the first earth saw his people and realized they were not very wise. They sat around all day with nothing to do. They wore no clothes and not a thing was done about it.

The creator decided to send a messenger to his people so that they might learn how to take care of themselves. The messenger was a spirit but came to the people in the form of a man. He saw that the people in the warm southern regions did not need clothes, so he left them alone. But in the north, the weather grew cold and the people were suffering. "Why are you sitting here with no clothing?" he asked.

The people of the first world looked confused. "What else can we do?" they asked.

The messenger began teaching the people how to make fire with a bow and stick. Then he showed them how to boil and cook meat with fresh birch bark. He gave them corn and helped them grow it. The messenger made their lives more comfortable than ever before.

The messenger thought of new ways to help his people. He shared the knowledge of dreams with them. "If you pay attention to your dreams," he said, "you will learn even more. But you must live good lives and keep your minds clear."

So the first people began to listen to their dreams and gained great things, like learning how to raise their children and heal the sick.

Group Project

Copper Scrolls

The Chippewa are well-known for their picture writing. They wrote their songs, legends, dances, and historical records on birch bark, stone, and wood. They even mined local copper and pounded or engraved it to make scrolls.

Materials (for each student)

- thin copper sheet, 5 x 7 inches (12.5 x 17.5 cm) OR oak tag
- shellac
- large nail
- sharpened pencil
- hammer
- rawhide lacing or twine
- permanent markers: black, red, brown, yellow
- wooden dowel
- ruler
- India Ink

To Make Designs in Copper

(Skip to step 4 if you are using oak tag.)

1. Sketch a symbol onto 5 x 7-inch (12.5 cm x 17.5 cm) newsprint.

2. Lay sketch over copper sheet. Etch the design into the copper by tracing over it with a sharpened pencil. (Figure 1)

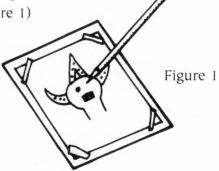

Figure 1

3. Remove sketch. Paint imprint with a layer of India ink. Blot excess. (Ink will remain in the etched grooves.) Let dry.

4. If you are using oak tag, draw design with permanent ink. Let dry. Coat design with clear shellac to give it a coppery sheen.

To Make Scrolls

5. Make three marks along the sides of each panel where it will be laced to other panels. Marks should be about 2 inches (5 cm) apart and an inch (2.5 cm) from the top and bottom edges of the panel.

6. Punch holes through the copper with hammer and nail; use a hole punch for oak tag. (Figure 2)

7. Lace panels together with twine or rawhide, in correct story sequence.

8. Place one dowel against the edge of the first panel. Roll copper or oak tag around dowel. Lace twine around scroll and knot loose ends. Repeat for the last panel. (Figure 3)

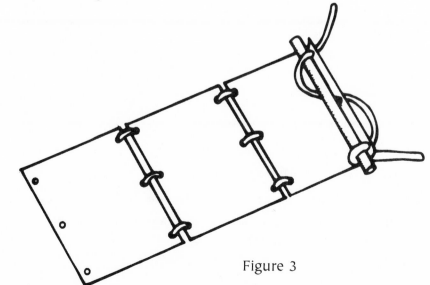

Figure 3

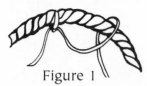

Figure 1

Figure 2

Figure 3

Figure 4

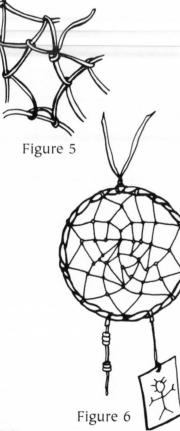

Figure 5

Figure 6

Individual Project

Dream Catcher
(Chippewa)

The Chippewa believed great wisdom and knowledge could come from dreams. Before going to bed each night, Indian parents would remind their children to remember their dreams.

Dream catchers, or spider-web charms, were placed on every infant's cradle. Any bad dreams would be caught by the web before they reached the sleeping child.

Materials (for one dream catcher)

– metal macramé hoop, about 4 inches (10 cm) in diameter
– leather lacing, about 18 (45 cm) inches
– waxed string, about 3 feet (1 meter)
– scissors
– rubber cement
– feathers
– small personal items such as photographs, trading cards, or beads

1. Wrap the leather lacing all the way around the macramé hoop. Tuck the end back into the lacing; secure the end with glue.

2. Tie a piece of the string to the hoop, then make a loose loop. (Figure 1)

3. Wrap the string around the hoop, tying off a loop at 1-inch (2.5 cm) increments. Do *not* cut the string. (Figure 2)

4. Continue all the way around until you reach the first loop again. Tie off a knot in the middle of the first loop and each loop that follows to form a second row of loops. (Figure 3)

5. Continue making loose loops until you have completed five or six rows. (Figure 4)

6. After reaching the center of the "web," pull the string tightly, then knot and cut. (Figure 5)

7. Tie one strip of leather around the top of the dream catcher for hanging. Tie the other two strips of leather at the bottom of the hoop for hanging personal articles. (Figure 6)

14

Native Americans of the Far North

Chippewa Scrolls

Because the Chippewa lacked a written language, they used pictographs as memory aids. The scrolls were passed on from one generation to the next. When the scrolls dried out or fell apart, it was up to each member of the tribe to accurately re-record the message.

The Chippewa believed that their family clans came from animals—also known as totems. Families were often depicted as animals in pictographs.

Native Americans of the Far North

Costumes to Color

Color the traditional garments by following the key below.

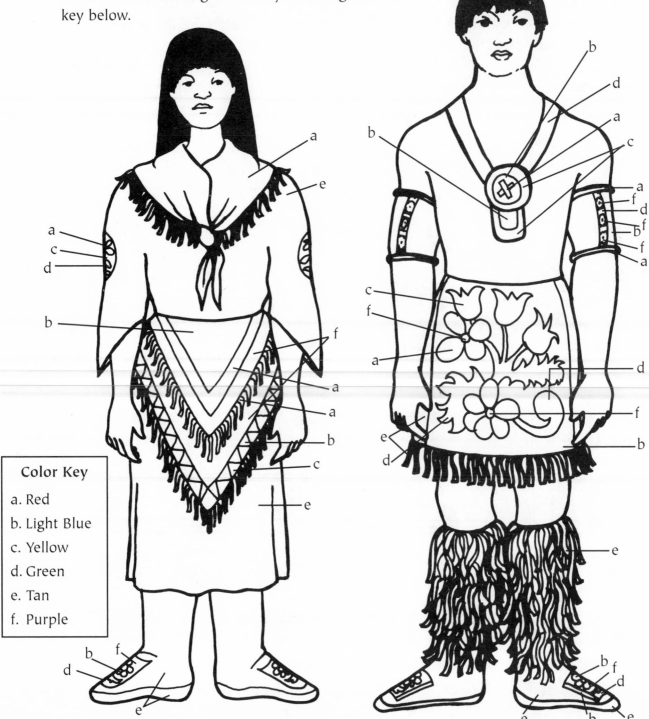

Color Key

a. Red

b. Light Blue

c. Yellow

d. Green

e. Tan

f. Purple

(Teacher's note: Use this page as a flat coloring sheet or enlarge each item to use in one of the special projects described on pages 7-8.)

Native Americans of the Far North

Tools and Dwellings to Color
(Chippewa)

Color each item by using the key below.

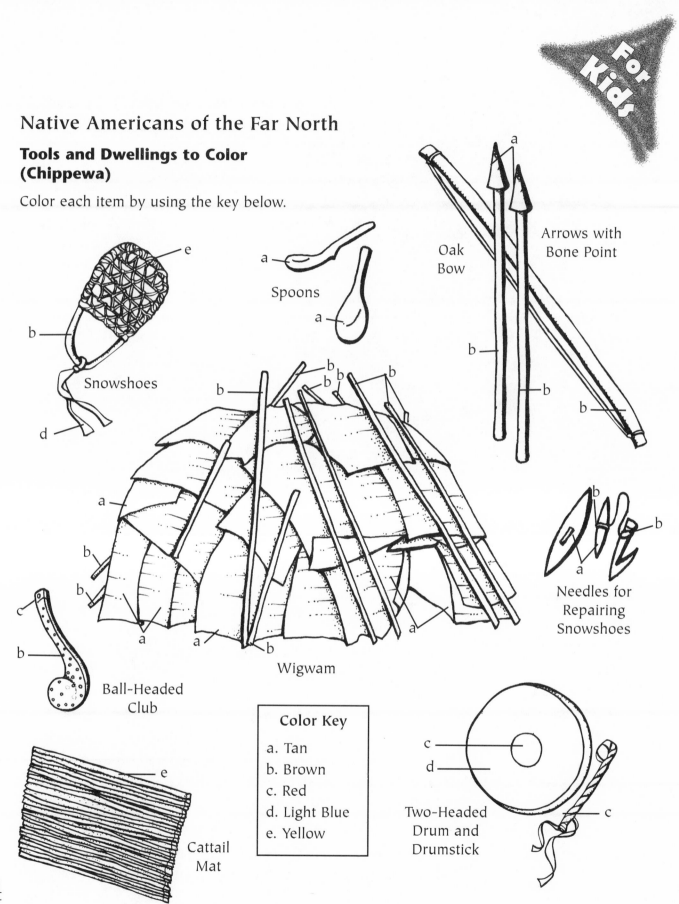

Snowshoes

Spoons

Oak Bow

Arrows with Bone Point

Wigwam

Needles for Repairing Snowshoes

Ball-Headed Club

Color Key

a. Tan
b. Brown
c. Red
d. Light Blue
e. Yellow

Two-Headed Drum and Drumstick

Cattail Mat

(Teacher's note: Use this page as a flat coloring sheet or enlarge each item to use in one of the special projects described on pages 7-8.)

Native Americans of the Eastern Woodlands

Background Information

The Woodland Indians lived in the area that stretches from the Great Lakes to the eastern seaboard and down to the southern regions of the Mississippi River.

The main Indian group living in this region was the **Iroquois.** Smaller tribes of the Iroquois Nation were the **Mohawks, Oneidas, Onondagas, Cayugas, Senecas, Hurons,** and **Tuscaroras.**

Iroquois
Husk Mask

How They Survived

Woodland Indians hunted for beaver, otter, moose, and bear. They also grew corn, beans, squash, and tobacco and harvested the wild rice that grew in the region's many lakes. To add sweetness to their foods, they collected sap, a sugary liquid produced by maple trees. Sap was made into syrup and candy.

The Iroquois tribes lived in buildings called longhouses. These huge structures, which were made from ash or cedar wood, were divided into small apartments for different family groups.

Making War, Making Peace

For centuries the different Iroquois tribes fought against each other. War was seen as an honorable way of life, and warriors in these tribes were greatly respected. Some Iroquois were cannibals, which means they occasionally ate their dead enemies.

In the sixteenth century, Deganawida, a member of the fierce Huron tribe, made his way into Iroquois territory to spread the

FACT

Many Northeastern Indians treated grandmothers as the most honored members of the tribe.

message of peace, but he was ignored. Then one day he met the Onandaga warrior, Hiawatha. Together, Deganawida and Hiawatha developed 13 laws to help the Iroquois get along better. This code of justice was known as the Great Law of Peace. The rights of the people included freedom of speech and freedom of religion. Women were also given the right to participate in government.

The Peacemaker chose a white pine tree to be the new symbol of the Iroquois, calling it the Tree of Peace. The council, chief statesmen, and clan leaders would sit under this tree and try to solve their problems together. They would vote on matters that were important to their people and agree on laws and rules. The decisions they made were recorded in Hiawatha's wampum belt. It was woven with symbols and images to remind people of tribal traditions.

Later, Benjamin Franklin visited the Iroquois and was impressed by their special government. He brought their ideas of democracy, in which people make decisions together, back to the leaders of the new country. The founding fathers used many of these ideals in forming their own government.

New Trading Partners, New Problems

During the seventeenth century, French traders began exploring Iroquois territory. They exchanged guns, metal axes, and tools with the Indians for the beaver fur that was so popular back in Europe. Seventy years later, beaver and other animals had become nearly extinct. In order to find food, the Iroquois had to move into territories controlled by other Indian groups. Many wars broke out as a result.

> **FACT**
>
> Many Woodland Indians punched holes in the soles of childrens' moccasins so that they would always walk close to the earth.

Wampum Beads

During the Revolutionary War the Iroquois tried not to take the side of either the British or the Americans. But some tribes took pity on General Washington's starving army at Valley Forge and gave them food and other supplies. Other groups began to help the British. The Iroquois League began to fall apart.

It was not until more than 100 years later that the tribes, living mostly on reservations (small sections of land set aside by the U.S. government) in the Northeast, decided to unite once again.

Wampum Belt

FACT

Northeastern Indians may have traded with other Native Americans as far away as the Rocky Mountains and the Gulf of Mexico.

Hiawatha and the Peacemaker (Iroquois)

In the ancient days a boy was born to the Huron tribe. His name was Deg-a-na-wida, which means "peacemaker" in Algonquin. Deganawida's grandmother dreamed that this child was born to bring peace to the people.

When he became a man, Peacemaker built a great canoe and set out on his peace mission. The Peacemaker met a woman. They shared a meal together. He explained his ideas about helping people get along. The woman said, "Your message is good but it will mean nothing if it does not take form."

The Peacemaker thought about what the woman said. "This peace must take the form of a longhouse with several fires for every family," he decided. "They will live under one roof and be guided under one chief. Five nations will have one fire and one mind."

The woman was the first to accept the new peace into her heart. Because of this, the Peacemaker promised that women would be allowed to act as chiefs.

The Peacemaker then went to a cannibal's house. He looked into the cannibal's face and saw it was good. He spoke to the man so that he might change his ways. The man accepted the news and they shared a meal of venison, or deer meat. The Peacemaker gave this man the name Hiawatha.

One day an evil man caused Hiawatha's family to die. Hiawatha was so filled with grief that he stopped speaking. He walked until he came to a lake. Some ducks helped him cross the lake by flapping their wings until the water lifted off the land.

Hiawatha found some shells in the dry lake bottom. He threaded them together to make a string of shells called wampum. Every night he repeated words of peace to comfort himself—one special word for each shell on the wampum belt.

The Peacemaker overheard Hiawatha's words and added strings of his own. The grief was lifted from Hiawatha's heart. Together the Peacemaker and Hiawatha created the Tree of Peace and talked words of healing into the wampum.

Group Project

Tree of Peace

Before You Begin

- Share *For Kids: Iroquois Tree of Peace* with students. Ask: *What does the Tree of Peace tell you about the Iroquois Nation?*
- Review the legend about Hiawatha and the Peacemaker as well as the historical information about the Iroquois government.
- Ask students to share their concerns about war and violence in our culture. Encourage children to discuss some of the strategies they use to solve everyday conflicts. Have them write paragraphs describing some of these strategies.

Materials

- white latex paint
- green tempera paint
- string
- pine cones
- photograph or self-portrait of each student

for the trunk
- cable spool (available from telephone companies)
- large tree limb (available at gardening centers) OR large cardboard carpet roll (available at carpet stores)
- large plastic bucket
- sand or gravel
- drill

for branches and evergreen clusters
- long sturdy twigs
- thin strips of balsa wood, about 5 inches (12.5 cm) long

To "Grow" a Classroom Tree

If you are using the tree limb . . .

1. If desired, attach additional branches to limb with strong masking tape.

2. Carefully paint tree and branches white. Let dry.

3. Insert tree inside the spool. (Figure 1)

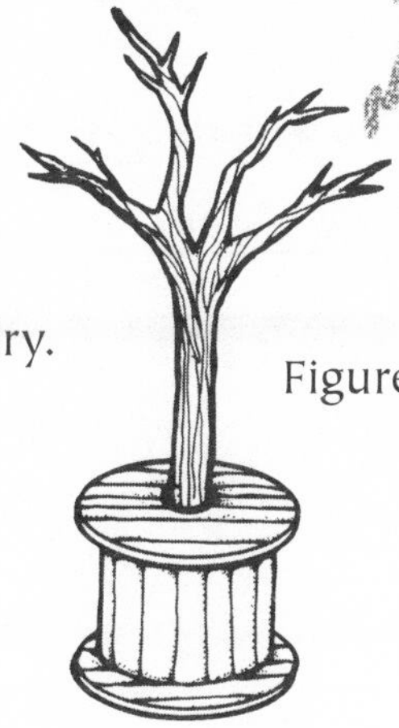

If you are using the carpet roll . . .

1. Build up branches by covering twigs with several layers of papier-mâché. Let dry.

2. Choose a drill bit that will enable you to insert branches into the tube. Drill holes all around the bottom of the tube, leaving about 6–12 inches (15–30 cm) at the bottom.

3. Paint branches and trunk white. Let dry.

4. Insert branches into trunk. (You may need to tape them from inside.)

5. Secure tree in the plastic container with sand or gravel. (Figure 2)

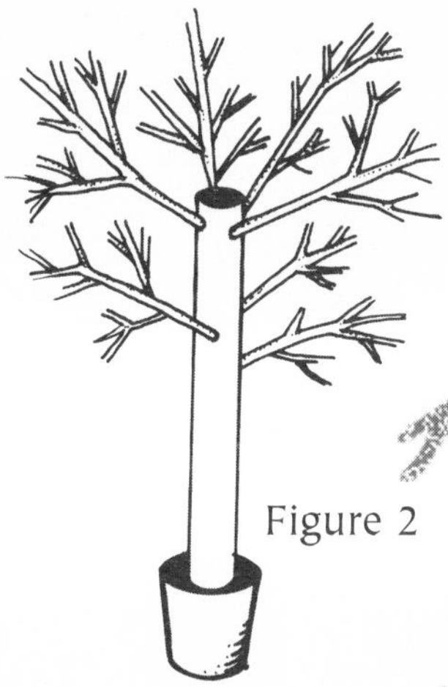

To Add the Pine Needles and Other Details

6. Paint balsa wood green. Let dry.

7. Glue balsa on the tree in clusters. (Figure 3)

8. Tie pine cones onto the tree. (Figure 4)

9. Tie the feathers at the top of the tree to represent the eagle.

10. Mount students' photos, along with their peacemaking strategies, onto green construction paper. Punch a hole at the top of each one and add string for hanging. After students read their conflict resolution strategies aloud, help children tie their papers onto the tree.

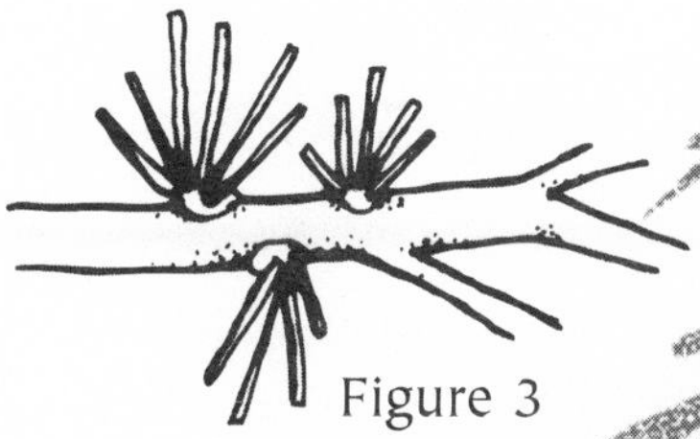

Figure 1

Figure 2

Figure 3

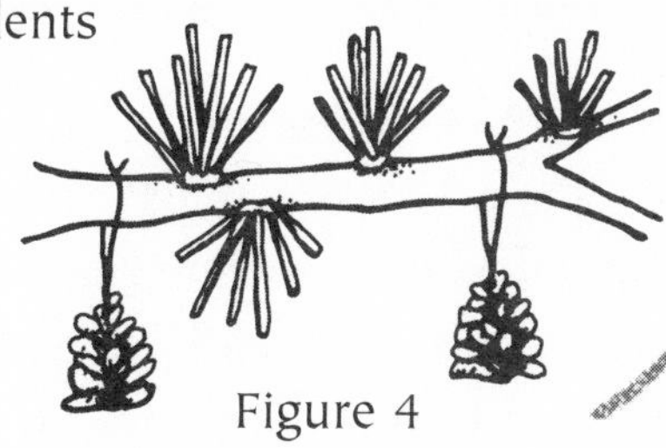

Figure 4

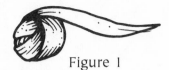

Figure 1

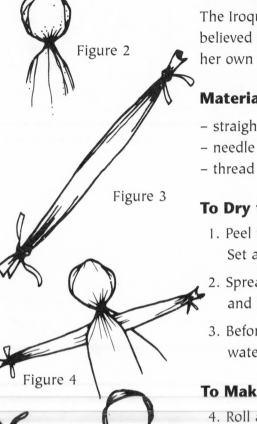

Figure 2

Figure 3

Figure 4

Figure 5

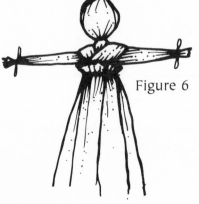

Figure 6

Individual Project

Cornhusk Doll

The Iroquois never painted faces on their cornhusk dolls. They believed that the corn god would provide each child with his or her own vision of what the doll should look like.

Materials

– straight pins
– needle
– thread

– 10 cornhusks per child OR paper "husk" ribbon, available in craft stores

To Dry the Husks

1. Peel the husks off the corn. Save the corn silk to use as hair. Set aside the corn to roast and sample later.

2. Spread the husks on a flat surface away from direct sunlight and let them air-dry.

3. Before making the dolls, soften the husks by soaking in warm water for 24 hours.

To Make the Doll's Head

4. Roll a few husks into a tight ball, approximately 1 inch (2.5 cm) in diameter. (Figure 1)

5. Layer another husk around the ball; twist. Tie off head area with thread. Allow husk ends to dangle freely. (Figure 2)

To Make Arms and Shoulders

6. Tie both ends of a piece of husk with thread. (Figure 3)

7. Insert the tied husk between the two dangling ends made by forming the head. (Figure 4)

8. Wrap two husks around the shoulder region of the doll, just below the head. (Figure 5) Pin the husks in place.

To Make the Waist

9. Tie thread around waist, just underneath shoulders.

10. Build waist region and rest of torso, by adding more husks. Use more thread to further define waist. (Figure 6)

11. Trim around bottom edge so doll can stand upright.

24

Native Americans of the Eastern Woodlands

Iroquois Tree of Peace

The Tree of Peace is an evergreen, which represents the continuing cycles of life. Here is what the rest of the tree represents.

Needle clusters are each family; **needles** represent each person in that family.

Each **branch** stands for the individual clans that are sheltered by the law of peace.

The white **roots** point to the four cardinal directions of the earth: North, South, East, and West.

The **eagle** represents the need to guard this peace at all times.

Pine cones carry seeds; they stand for generations to come.

The **trunk** represents the strength of the nation and the unity of its people.

The many **weapons** buried under the tree's roots are a promise not to make war.

When you have problems with friends or family members, what kinds of peacemaking strategies do you use to solve them? _____

_____

_____

_____

© 1997 Good Apple

25

Native Americans of the Eastern Woodlands

Costumes to Color

Color the traditional garments by following the key below.

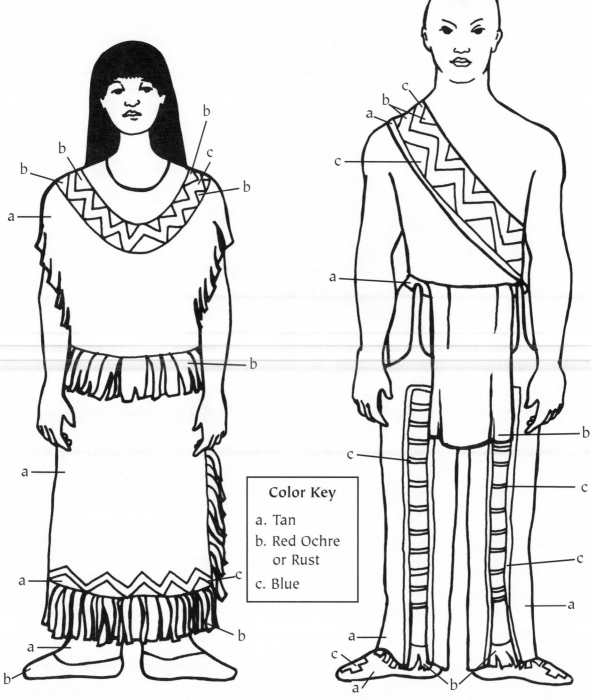

Color Key

a. Tan

b. Red Ochre or Rust

c. Blue

(Teacher's note: Use this page as a flat coloring sheet or enlarge each item to use in one of the special projects described on pages 7-8.)

Native Americans of the Eastern Woodlands

Tools and Dwellings to Color
(Iroquois)

Color the tools and dwellings by following the key below.

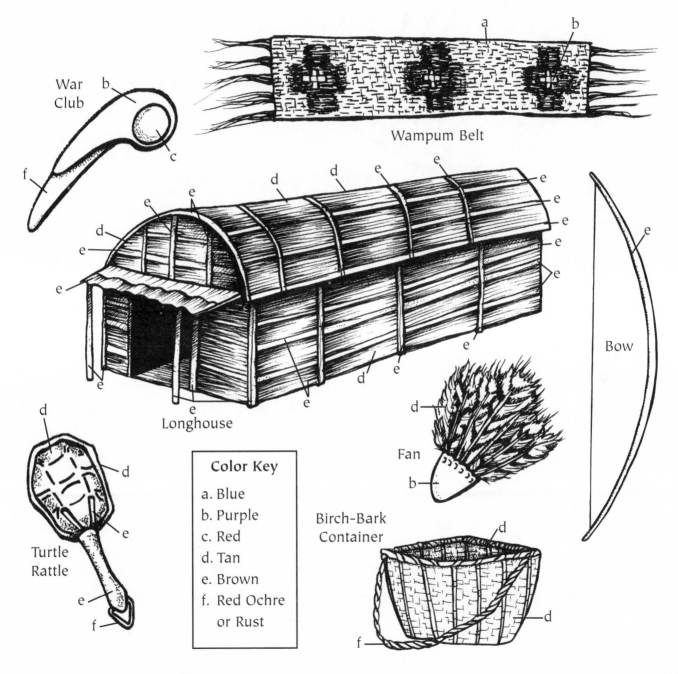

War Club

Wampum Belt

Longhouse

Bow

Fan

Turtle Rattle

Color Key

a. Blue
b. Purple
c. Red
d. Tan
e. Brown
f. Red Ochre
   or Rust

Birch-Bark Container

(Teacher's note: Use this page as a flat coloring sheet or enlarge each item to use in one of the special projects described on pages 7-8.)

Native Americans of the Southeast

Background Information

The land of the southeastern Indians stretched across the Mississippi River to the Atlantic coast, north to the Ohio River, and south to the Gulf of Mexico.

The largest southeastern tribes included the **Cherokee, Creek, Chickasaw, Choctaw, Natchez,** and **Seminole.** The ancestors of most of these people are called the Mississippian culture, or Mound Builders. They lived in the region from about 1000 B.C. to A.D. 700. The huge mounds they built rise as high as 100 feet. Some mounds cover an area of more than five square miles!

People who study ancient civilizations believe that some of the mounds might have been used as temples and that others were used for burials.

Seminole Hole-and-Slot Heddle for Woven Beadwork

How They Survived

Southeastern Indians grew corn, beans, squash, sunflowers, and tobacco. They also grew gourds to use as bowls, spoons, and other utensils. Some of the animals these Native Americans hunted were deer, bear, turkey, buffalo, and rabbit. Hunting tools included bows and arrows, masks, decoys, and spears to hunt for wild game. Southeastern tribes also hunted with darts filled with a poison made from chestnuts, walnuts, locusts, and other materials.

During the winter many southeastern Native Americans lived in small cone-shaped houses called *asis*. These buildings were made of sticks and poles. The walls were covered in claylike mud called wattle. During the summer the people lived in rectangular homes with open walls and roofs made of bark and grass.

FACT

Some southeastern Indians placed small bags of sand against their babies' foreheads. This caused the babies' heads to flatten, which was considered a sign of beauty.

Everyday Customs and Beliefs

The most important festival of the year for many southeastern tribes was the Green Corn Dance, which took place in August. Before the ceremony, all the people cleaned their homes. All the fires in the houses were put out. There was a day of fasting followed by a great feast day. This was a time when many crimes were forgiven. At the end of the festival, everyone would take a bath to purify themselves for the upcoming year.

In the 1700s, the Cherokee adopted many of the customs of the European settlers. They built their homes into log houses and began to use cotton cloth instead of deerskin to make their clothing. Later, a Cherokee man named Sequoyah developed the first Cherokee alphabet. Within a few months the Indians learned to read and write in their own language.

The Spanish Bring Change

The Spanish conquistadors, or conquerors, landed in Florida in 1513. They captured many of the Indians to sell as slaves in Cuba and the West Indies. Those Indians who fought back were often killed. The few surviving Indians joined with the **Seminoles**, a tribe made up of escaped slaves and Indians from other tribes. In fact, the word *seminole* means "runaway."

Over time other groups of Indians tried to live peacefully with the European settlers. Many became farmers and raised cattle and sheep. Others became plantation owners. The Cherokees, Seminoles, Choctaws, Creeks, and Chickasaws came to be known by the Europeans as the Five Civilized Tribes.

Cherokee
Blowgun

FACT

In 1828 the first Indian newspaper, *The Cherokee Phoenix*, was published in both English and Cherokee.

The Trail of Tears

For a while the southeastern Indians and the settlers got along. But new problems soon developed. The plantation owners wanted Indian lands for raising tobacco and cotton. The tribes refused to give up their territory—at first.

Over time the southeastern tribes were forced off their lands. From 1831 to 1835 the Choctaw and Cherokee were herded together and forced to walk thousands of miles west to reservations in Oklahoma. Thousands of Indians died from the freezing temperatures, starvation, and disease. The Indians called this forced march The Trail of Tears. The lands they found when they arrived on the reservations were often poor for farming.

The Creeks, on the other hand, held out longer against the settlers. They went to war against the white plantation owners. But they lost and were forced to move to reservations in western Arkansas. By that time the remaining southeastern tribes felt they would not win if they challenged the white settlers. They gave up without a fight, and almost all of them were sent to reservations.

Seminole
Mortar &
Pestle

How the Milky Way Was Made (Cherokee)

Each night the Cherokee people locked their food into a storehouse. But one morning they discovered some of it had been stolen. They looked around to find some clues, thinking that an enemy tribe had snuck in during the night. Instead, they found huge paw prints all around the storehouse.

Some of the people were frightened, saying such a large animal must be a monster. After a long discussion about what to do, one old man said, "Monster or not, we must stop this creature from eating up our supplies. I have a plan."

The people listened to the old man's plan. "Everyone will get their rattles and other noisemakers and meet here tonight," he explained. "Then we will hide around the storehouse and wait for this beast to come. I will signal you when I see him and we will frighten him away with a great noise."

That night the whole village gathered with their rattles and drums. The people crouched low in the shadows and patiently waited. Much later a giant dog appeared from the west. At first the old man was too frightened to do anything. But as he watched the dog begin to take great gulps of food, he was able to gather his courage to sound the alarm.

The entire village rose up. The people shook their rattles, beat their drums, and screamed. They began to surround the dog, who became frightened and confused. He ran around and around in a circle, then leapt high into the sky. The meal that was in his mouth poured out and made a white trail across the darkness.

The Cherokee call this trail *Where the Dog Ran*. Other people call this trail in the sky *The Milky Way*.

Group Project

Booger Masks

Cherokee Booger Dance

During the winter the Cherokees hold a special ceremony called the Booger Dance. The dance is hosted by one member of the community. The villagers gather with their drums and rattles and wait for the festivities to begin.

Four people enter the host's home wearing masks painted with ridiculous facial expressions. The host asks, "Who are you?" The dancers reply that they are from far away. They begin to dance around and tease the guests. The dance is not meant to frighten people but to help them realize that, if they stay together as a group, they have little to fear from their enemies.

The original booger masks were made of carved wood and painted with natural dyes. Strips of fur were used for hair. Many of the masks represented European settlers and other Cherokee enemies.

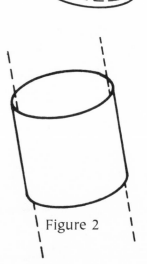

Figure 1

Materials

- liquid starch
- newspaper
- plastic bleach bottle (makes 2 masks)
- sturdy scissors
- tempera paints
- thin string, elastic, or cord
- fake fur and feathers

To Make the Mask Base

1. Cut off the bottom and top of the bottle and remove the handle. (Figure 1)

2. Cut the bottle in half to make two curved mask bases. (Figure 2)

Figure 2

3. Punch large holes for eyes in the fronts of the masks and smaller holes for inserting string on the sides of the masks. (Figure 3)

Figure 3

To Make Faces

4. Tear enough strips of newspaper to cover the outside of the mask.

5. Saturate individual newspaper strips with liquid starch and lay them on top of the mask base. Continue until the mask is completely covered except for the eye holes. (Figure 4)

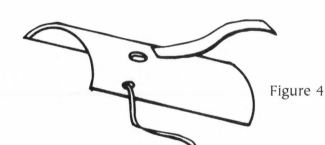

Figure 4

6. To make noses or mouths, wad up some saturated newspaper strips and mold them into desired shapes. (The sillier the better!)

7. Once the masks have dried, paint them and add fake fur and feathers.

8. Insert cord or string through the holes.

Individual Project

Gourd Rattles

The Cherokee used many musical instruments for their dances, ceremonies, and festivals. Rattles were used to summon people to participate in the dances. Most of the rattles were made of turtle shells. Later the Cherokee used gourds.

Materials

– dried gourds, available in nursery supply centers or florists OR evaporated milk containers, cleaned and rinsed
– popcorn kernels or pebbles
– 12 inch (30 cm) length of 1/2-inch (1.25 cm) dowel

If you are using a can
• Wash and dry the can thoroughly.
• Spray paint the can light brown, tan, or yellow ochre. Proceed with the directions below.

To Make the Rattles

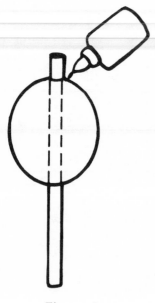

Figure 1

1. If you are using a gourd, drill in each side a hole large enough for the dowel. If you are using a can, make holes in each end with a can opener. Enlarge the holes with the can opener so that the dowel will fit.

2. Plug one hole with your finger and insert a few pebbles or popcorn kernels into the other hole. To test the rattle's sound, cover both holes and shake the rattle. Add or subtract kernels or pebbles until you achieve the desired sound effect.

3. Push the dowel through one hole and out the other side, allowing at least 2 inches (5 cm) of the dowel to stick out on each side. Glue the dowel in place. (Figure 1)

4. Paint rattles with some of the designs suggested on page 35. Tie leather to the handle and decorate with feathers and beads.

Native Americans of the Southeast

Rattles and Masks

Medicine men were in charge of making rattles. As they made them, the medicine men would pray that the rattles would be given their own special "voices."

Cherokee women wore rattles on their legs for night ceremonies. These dancers were called shell-shaker girls.

Native Americans of the Southeast

Costumes to Color

Color the traditional garments by following the
key below.

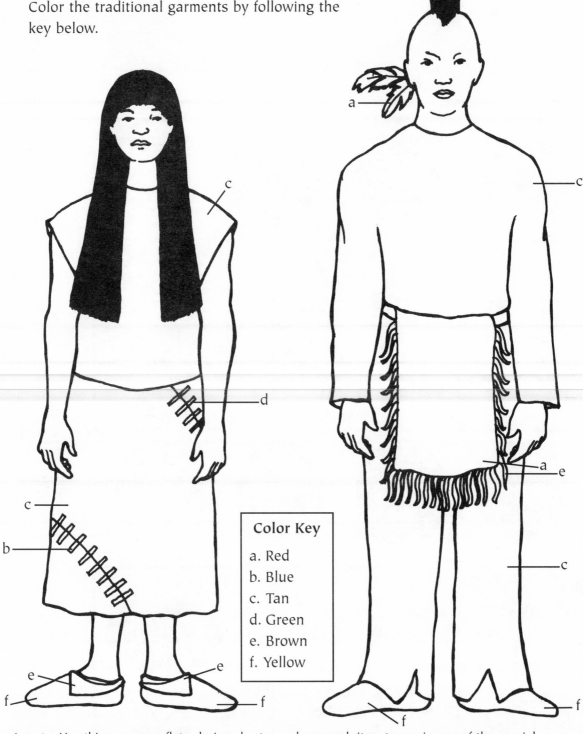

Color Key

a. Red
b. Blue
c. Tan
d. Green
e. Brown
f. Yellow

(Teacher's note: Use this page as a flat coloring sheet or enlarge each item to use in one of the special
projects described on pages 7-8.)

Native Americans of the Southeast

Tools and Dwellings to Color

Color each item by using the key below.

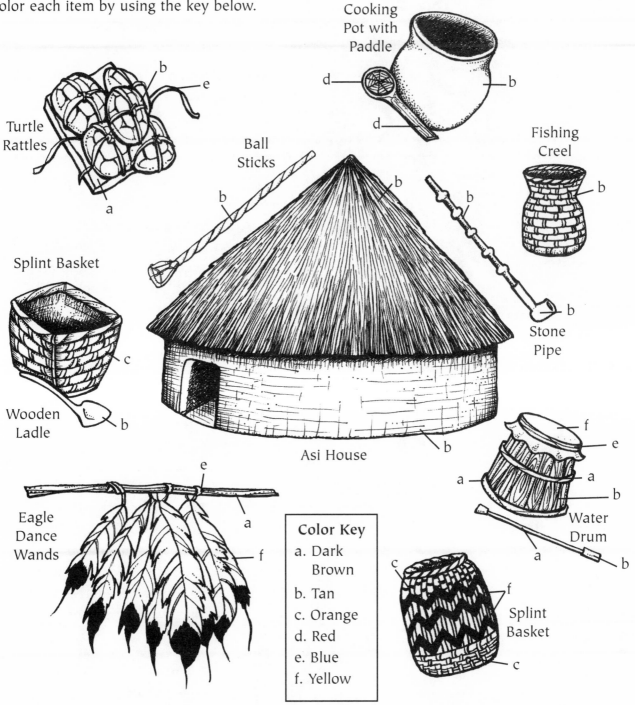

Cooking
Pot with
Paddle

d

b

d

Fishing
Creel

b

Turtle
Rattles

b

e

a

Ball
Sticks

b

b

b

b

Stone
Pipe

Splint Basket

c

Wooden
Ladle

b

Asi House

b

f

e

a

a

b

Water
Drum

a

b

Eagle
Dance
Wands

e

a

f

c

f

Splint
Basket

c

Color Key
a. Dark
   Brown
b. Tan
c. Orange
d. Red
e. Blue
f. Yellow

(Teacher's note: Use this page as a flat coloring sheet or enlarge each item to use in one of the special projects described on pages 7-8.)

Native Americans of the Great Plains

Background Information

The Plains Indians lived in the middle part of North America, a vast land of sun, wind, and grass that covered over half a billion acres. The territory of the Plains Indians spread east to the Mississippi River, west to the Rocky Mountain foothills, north into Canada's Saskatchewan River, and south to the Rio Grande. At one point there were over 63 major tribes living on the Plains. Some of the larger groups were the **Sioux** nation **(Nakota, Lakota, Dakota)**, as well as the **Blackfoot, Pawnee, Crow, and Comanche.**

How They Survived

These Indians were nomadic, following the animals they hunted from place to place. The most important source of food for Plains Indians was the millions of buffaloes roaming the territory. The Indians used every bit of the buffaloes they killed. The hides were used for clothing, tipis, shields, and drums. The bones were made into tools, eating utensils, necklaces, and decorations on headdresses. Even the dung was turned into fuel for campfires!

Spanish settlers introduced the Plains Indians to horses in the 1700s. As they became better

War Bonnet

FACT

The Spanish explorers introduced the Plains Indians to tamed horses.

riders, Native Americans used horses to roam even more widely over the plains, sometimes invading the territories of their neighbors. Wars began to break out. As war became a way of life, warriors became honored members of the tribe.

The Buffaloes Begin to Disappear

The Plains Indians and European settlers had a friendly relationship until the 1800s. But soon buffalo hides became very popular in Europe, so white hunters began slaughtering, or killing in huge numbers, whole herds, skinning the animals and leaving the meat to rot in the sun. The Native Americans were horrified by this wastefulness. By the turn of the century, the buffalo was nearly extinct.

Americans began leaving their cities on the East Coast and settling in the Great Plains. They ignored the treaties, or agreements, that protected Indian territory. They often built their homes on Indian land, right in the paths of migrating animals. Railroad tracks and telegraph lines began to crisscross the countryside. As the animals that the Indians had once hunted were killed off or were scared away, the Indians began to starve to death.

Plains Indians, like Native Americans everywhere, caught the diseases carried by the Europeans. Their bodies did not have the chemicals, or antibodies, that would protect them from such diseases, and many died.

Buffalo
Headress

Solving Problems With the Settlers

The Plains Indians were troubled by what they saw. Should they fight the invading settlers with arrows and hatchets, or should they try to make better treaties? Some Indians attacked and fought against the United States Army; others tried to make new agreements with government leaders.

But nothing seemed to work. In the middle of the 1800s, new wars broke out. Indians were forced to live on reservations, small sections of land set aside by the U.S. government. These lands were usually poor for farming and difficult for everyday living. Indian children were often sent to boarding schools, where they were forced to give up their religious beliefs, their tribal customs, and even their language.

Counting
Stick

White Feather and the Giant
(Sioux)

Chacopee was a famous warrior who wore a magic white feather in his hair. One day a cruel giant of the forest tricked him, stole the white feather, and changed the young warrior into a dog. The giant then put the feather in his own hair.

The dog and the giant traveled to a village where two daughters of a chief lived. Both girls had heard of the magical warrior with the white feather. Upon seeing the giant, the older daughter invited him into her lodge and the younger girl took the dog into her home.

One day both the giant and Chacopee went hunting. Chacopee threw a stone into the water. Suddenly the stone turned into a beaver, which the dog quickly caught and killed. The giant tried the same magic, but by the time he got home, the beaver had turned back into a stone.

The chief heard about all this and grew curious. He invited both the dog and giant for a visit so could see the magic himself. But, instead of a dog, a very handsome warrior greeted him. It was Chacopee! Although he was no longer a dog, he still could not speak.

A tribal meeting was held for this special occasion. Each warrior took a puff from the welcoming pipe. Chacopee took the pipe, and the smoke formed into a flock of pigeons. At that very moment, the young man was able to speak again. He told the chief how the giant had tricked him. The chief was furious and ordered that the giant be turned into a dog.

Chacopee was grateful. He took a buffalo hide and cut it into tiny pieces. Then he tossed the pieces over the flat, empty prairie. The hides grew into a magnificent buffalo herd, which the warriors were invited to hunt.

Group Project

Ceremonial Hide Blanket

Storytelling Pictographs

The Plains Indians often drew pictographs, or symbols standing for words, on hides. The pictographs tell stories of great adventures or acts of bravery. The Indians sometimes used these decorated hides to make ceremonial blankets for honored guests.

Before You Begin

- Share *For Kids: Pictographs and Shield Symbols*. Look at and discuss the individual pictographs and the pictograph story. Ask students to devise their own messages with pictographs, then challenge partners to decipher them.

- Work together as a class to think of a recent adventure or event you and your students have shared. Summarize the story so that it can be described in 20 pictographs, depending on the size of your blanket (see Materials list below).

- Assign each student the responsibility of designing one pictograph symbol onto a hide. Remind them that they can make up their own pictograph symbols if necessary.

Materials (for each blanket)

– 20 large brown paper bags
(NOTE: If you have a large class, give each student the opportunity to contribute a pictograph by increasing the size of the blanket by multiples of four.)
– scissors
– markers or crayons: black, white, blue, green, yellow, brown

To Make Hides

1. Cut down the main seam of the bag; cut out the bottom panel. Set scraps aside. Crumple the paper until it becomes soft and supple.

2. Alternatively (for more realistic "leather") soak bags in water until glue dissolves and bags open. Crumple bags tightly to squeeze out excess water. Flatten bags and let dry.

Figure 1

3. Draw your pictograph onto the "hide." (Figure 1)

To Sew the Blanket

4. Use a ruler, pencil, and hole punch to make three evenly spaced holes, 1 inch (2.5cm) from the edge of each bag. (Use the same measurements for each bag.)

5. Lay 20 hides together on the floor, in rows four across and five down, to form a rectangle. Make sure symbols appear in correct story sequence, from left to right. (Figure 2)

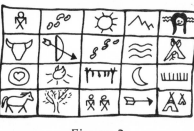

Figure 2

6. Use string or twine to lace the hides as closely together as possible. (Figure 3)

To Add a Border (optional)

Figure 3

7. Cut paper bag scraps into strips no more than 4 inches (10 cm) wide. (Lengths may vary.) Tape strips together to make one border measuring about 66 inches (165 cm) and two borders measuring 50 inches (125 cm) each.

8. Ask students to decorate borders with pictographs reflecting the history of the Plains Indians.

9. Attach borders by taping along the back edges of blankets.

43

Individual Project

Dance Shields

The Plains Indians painted their shields with designs that were both decorative and protective.

Materials (for each shield)

– chamois or tan cotton square, 28 x 28 inches
  (70 cm x 70 cm)
– quilter's hoop, 17 inches (42.5 cm) in diameter
– rawhide or plain string
– acrylic paint: black, blue, yellow, white, green, red
– brushes

To Make Dance Shields

1. Lay the quilter's hoop in the center of the cloth. Cut the cloth in a circular form about 6 inches (15 cm) larger than the diameter of the hoop.

2. Punch holes around the edges of the cloth.

3. Lace string in and out of the holes in a running stitch. Gather cloth to fit tightly over the hoop. (Figure 1)

4. Use pictographs and basic shield symbols as decorations.

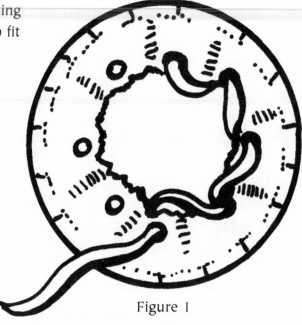

Figure 1

Native Americans of the Great Plains

Pictographs and Shield Symbols

The Plains Indians used pictographs to record important events. Each pictograph was like a word. When they were strung together, the pictographs made a whole story. This pictograph tells the story of two friends who went hunting for buffalo in the summer.

Here are some other pictograph symbols.

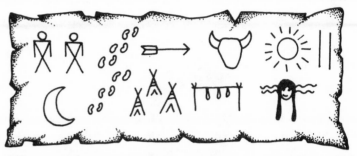

What It Means: The two warriors rested after they shot a buffalo with their arrows. In the evening they went back to their village for a feast and listened to many stories.

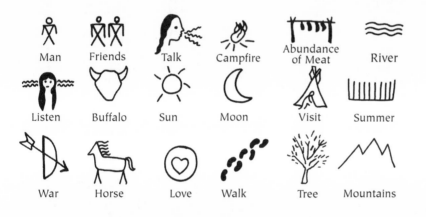

Man   Friends   Talk   Campfire   Abundance of Meat   River

Listen   Buffalo   Sun   Moon   Visit   Summer

War   Horse   Love   Walk   Tree   Mountains

Shields

One Dakota warrior painted his shield with an eagle to watch over him.

- The **four stars** were painted yellow for dawn, red for day, green for the sky, and black for night.

- The **lightning bolts** symbolize what it feels like to face death.

- The red **stripes** in the center shield represent the United States, the enemy of this warrior.

Native Americans of the Great Plains

Costumes to Color

Color the traditional garments by following the key below.

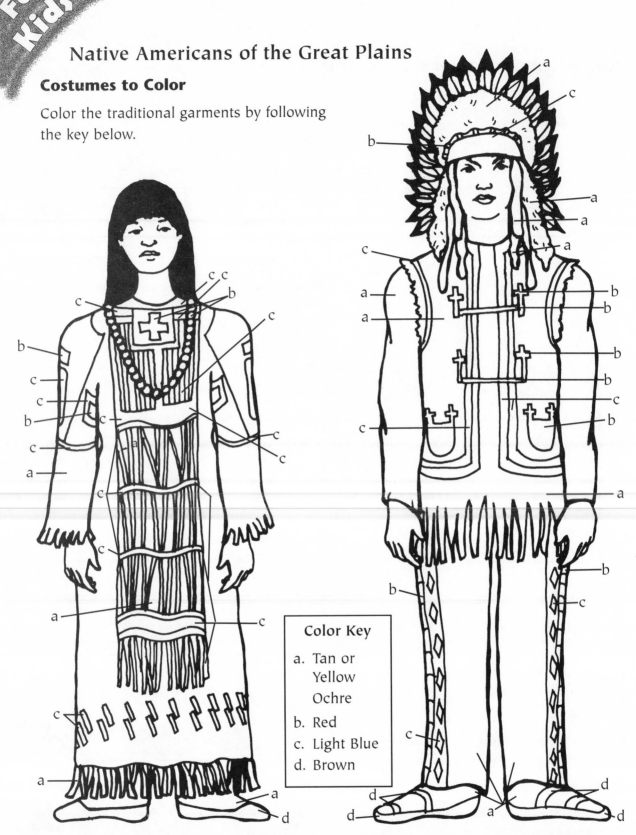

Color Key

a. Tan or Yellow Ochre

b. Red

c. Light Blue

d. Brown

(Teacher's note: Use this page as a flat coloring sheet or enlarge each item to use in one of the special projects described on pages 7-8.)

Native Americans of the Great Plains

Tools and Dwellings to Color

Color the tools and dwellings by following the key below.

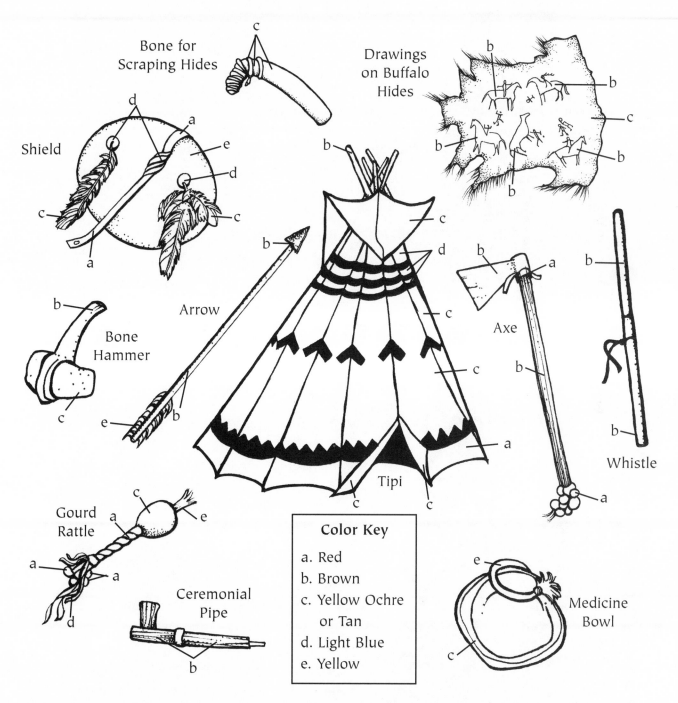

Bone for
Scraping Hides

Drawings
on Buffalo
Hides

Shield

Arrow

Bone
Hammer

Axe

Whistle

Tipi

Gourd
Rattle

Ceremonial
Pipe

Medicine
Bowl

Color Key

a. Red
b. Brown
c. Yellow Ochre
   or Tan
d. Light Blue
e. Yellow

(Teacher's note: Use this page as a flat coloring sheet or enlarge each item to use in one of the special projects described on pages 7-8.)

Native Americans of the Northwest Coast

Totem Pole

Background Information

The Northwest Coast Indians lived on the Pacific Rim of North America. This territory includes British Columbia, the land around the Columbia River, and up the Alaska panhandle. The coastline is rugged, broken up by many inlets and channels.

The major groups that settled in this area were the **Haida, Tlingit, Tsimshian, Nootka, Salish,** and **Kwakiutl tribes.**

How They Survived

The Northwest Indians hunted and trapped caribou, moose, sheep, goats, and small animals. They gathered edible roots and berries and used their boating skills to catch fish like salmon, candlefish, halibut, and herring. These fish were either eaten fresh or dried and stored. Other vitamin-filled foods from the sea included oysters, clams, whales, and sea lions.

Northwest Indians used sinew, a fiber made from sea lion bladders, in much the same way as rope. They made scraping and cutting tools from whale bones. The oil of the candlefish was used for lighting lamps.

The Indians lived in permanent villages close to the sea or its inlets. Their houses were made of cedar planks painted with animal and bird designs. In the summer the tribes left their villages and set up camps to harvest seafood. When winter approached the Indians would return home with baskets of dried fish and other foods.

FACT

The Northwest Indians may have traded with natives in Hawaii—more than 3,000 miles away!

During the cold winter months, the Indians spent their time weaving blankets, baskets, and mats from grass fibers and cedar bark. They also carved figures in wood and stone. Families gathered around the fire to tell stories and share dances based on clan legends.

Everyday Customs and Rituals

Important events such as the birth of a child, a marriage, or the raising of a totem pole were marked by a gift-giving ceremony called a potlatch. A family would invite hundreds of guests from neighboring clans, or large family groups, to this huge feast. The potlatch would last for days or sometimes even weeks. After the feast, gifts of canoes, blankets, and food were given away. The value of the gifts showed how generous the host families were. Guests would return the favor by holding their own potlatch ceremony soon afterwards, trying to prove that they were even more generous.

Totem poles were another important part of Northwest Coast culture. Only chiefs or the richest families could afford them. Each totem pole is a monument based on a family's history, much like a European coat of arms. The Northwest Indians believed that their oldest ancestors were mythological animals. Each design on the pole tells how an ancestor overcame a supernatural creature or changed into a human being.

Only special artists were allowed to create totem poles. A rich chief would hire the artist based on his experience, creativity, and knowledge of tribal history. It was believed that the carver was guided by the spirits of his own ancestors. Prayers and songs were dedicated to the spirits as a craftsman worked.

FACT

The ancestors of these and other Native Americans came to this continent from Asia at least 15,000 years ago.

Haida Double Whistle

Canoes, like totem poles, were status symbols that showed how rich and important a family was. A great amount of time and energy was spent finding the right tree to use for each new boat. Again, only the most skilled craftsmen were allowed to make canoes.

New Wealth, New Problems

There were many visitors to the Northwest Coast over the years, but it was the Englishman James Cook who made these Indians and their territory well-known. Cook recorded the Indians' customs and artwork, particularly totem poles, in his journals. He also traded knives and other tools for sea otter pelts to sell in other countries.

The local chiefs and tribes became wealthier as the rich natural resources of the area were slowly discovered by outsiders. Most of this wealth ended suddenly when trading in sea otter pelts was no longer popular.

Haida Canoe

How Raven Gave Earth Light
(Tlingit)

The god-chief, Nass-shikke-yahl, created all the creatures in the earth and sky. But he did not give them light, so both humans and animals stumbled around in the darkness for some time. People eventually learned to catch the candlefish, dry it out, and burn it in stone dishes for light. But the light this oil made was weak.

Raven was cunning but also compassionate. He saw that the lack of light was a problem and decided to play a trick on the god-chief. Raven knew that if he became the human grandson to Nass-shikke-yahl, he could have anything he wanted. So Raven changed himself into the needle from a hemlock tree and floated on the water. Nass-shikke-yahl's daughter took a drink and accidentally swallowed the needle.

The daughter now carried Raven inside of her and soon gave him a new life through birth. She gave Raven his grandfather's name and, as Raven had suspected, the great god-chief was very pleased.

Raven quickly put his plan into action. First he begged for the moon and, upon receiving it, threw it high into the sky. He did the same with the stars, and the heavens became full of light. The proud grandfather then gave Raven the most treasured gift of all, a box that contained the sun.

Raven went to the river bank where many people were fishing. They were loud and rude. Raven asked the people to be quiet. He threatened to open the box and make the sun shine on them. The people laughed because they did not believe that he held such a thing as sunshine or that he was the grandson of the god-chief.

Raven opened the sun box just a bit and lightning flew out onto the people like a storm. The fishermen were so frightened that they actually grew louder. That made Raven open the box all the way until light covered the entire land.

Group Project

Totem Pole
(Tlingit)

The Tlingit and other Northwest Coast Indians named themselves after animals important to ancestor myths and stories, such as the Raven Clan or Eagle Clan. Totem poles include symbols that explain the history of the mother's side of the family. Special events in the owner's life are also recorded on the poles.

Before you begin:

- Make copies of the *For Kids: Animal Totems* page. Ask students to point out features of designs that remind them of various animals. (You may want to share photographs of the real animals as you discuss totem designs.) What features of each animal did the totem carvers choose to exaggerate?

- Ask students: *What hopes and dreams do you have for your families? What stories are important to your families?*

Help students use real animal pictures to sketch animal totem designs that represent their families. Arrange them vertically as a point of comparison to the totems you will make, below.

Materials

- posterboard, one sheet per two students
- heavy white paper, 8 1/2 x 11 inches (22 cm x 27.5 cm); one per student
- tempera paints: red, black, light blue, tan, yellow, gray, and white
- wide black markers
- masking tape
- double-sided transparent tape
- scissors
- rubber cement
- white glue
- wood for totem pole base

To Make Totem Designs

1. Choose a design to copy from the *For Kids: Animal Totems* page. Use an opaque or overhead projector to enlarge the design and trace the picture onto white paper.

2. Trace over the lines of the design with black marker or paint. Let dry.

3. Use tempera paint to color in the white spaces of the design. Let dry.

To Make the Totem Pole

4. Roll each piece of posterboard into a cylinder. Tape the seams together. Wrap tape all the way around the cylinder to secure it firmly. (One cylinder will hold two totem designs.)

5. Tape cylinders together to make one long pole. (Figure 1)

Figure 1

6. Lay the pole on a surface protected with newspapers. Paint brown. Let pole dry overnight.

7. Use double-sided tape to carefully attach designs to the pole, leaving a 1-inch (2.5 cm) space along the bottom of the pole.

8. Add bold graphics and animal symbols with black paint.

9. After pole is completely dry, use masking tape to attach it to a cardboard or wooden base. (You may need several layers of tape so the pole will stand upright.) (Figure 2)

10. Use brown paint to disguise masking tape around the pole's base.

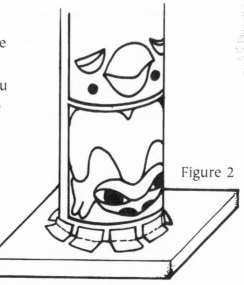

Figure 2

53

Individual Project

Plaster Carvings

The Northwest Coast Indians carved in both wood and soft soapstone. Their designs were used mainly for decoration and display and were based on animals representing clan groups.

Materials (per student)

- 1/2 cup plaster of Paris powder
- 3/4 cup vermiculite, an organic potting material found at gardening centers
- pint-size milk carton, rinsed and dried
- carbon paper

- 1/2 cup water
- stick
- small plastic bowl
- dull kitchen knife, nail, or other item with semi-sharp point

(NOTE: If stored in plastic bags, the vermiculite will keep the plaster soft enough to carve easily for up to two weeks.)

To Make Plaster Cast

1. Pour the plaster of Paris and vermiculite into a bowl. Slowly add water and stir until the mixture resembles thick gravy.

2. Transfer the mixture into a milk carton and let it set for 30 minutes.

3. While the plaster is drying, choose a totem design to carve. Use your photocopier to enlarge the design 125%.

4. Once the plaster has hardened, peel away the carton; lay the copied design over one side of the plaster block. (Figure 1)

5. Slip carbon paper underneath the design, shiny side against the plaster. Tape into place.

6. Trace each line by pressing hard with a pencil. Remove carbon sheet and design.

Figure 1

To Carve Design

7. Scrape off surrounding layers of plaster with a spoon or dull knife. (Figure 2)

8. Allow the plaster to dry for two or three more days, then add details by etching with a sharp pin or nail.

Figure 2

Native Americans of the Northwest Coast

Animal Totems

Each totem pole showed animals important to a family's history.

BEAR's spirit helps people perform great feats with skill and endurance.

RAVEN possesses the spirit of a fine hunter. He cleans the trash left by animals and careless people. People who carry this name must be clean and pure in their daily lives.

DOG is a great ancestral spirit who helps people become strong and fierce.

LOON gives women skills in weaving and sewing. He grants men powerful fishing skills.

FROG is a friend of Raven. He warns people of trouble from enemies. He also brings good fortune.

SEA OTTER helps people become skilled hunters and fishers. He also grants great wealth.

What animal totem might represent your family? Why?

Native Americans of the Northwest Coast

Costumes to Color

Color these traditional garments by following the key below.

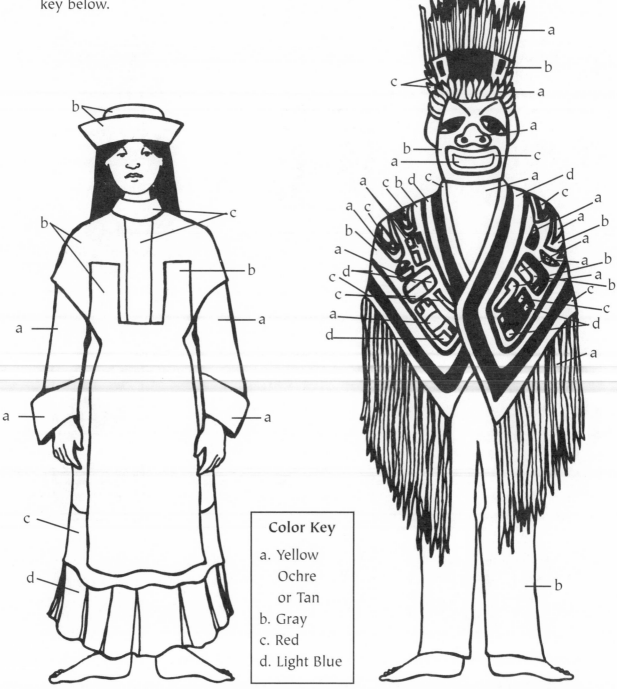

Color Key

a. Yellow
   Ochre
   or Tan
b. Gray
c. Red
d. Light Blue

(Teacher's note: Use this page as a flat coloring sheet or enlarge each item to use in one of the special projects described on pages 7-8.)

Native Americans of the Northwest Coast

Tools and Dwellings to Color
(Tlingit)

Color each item by using the key below.

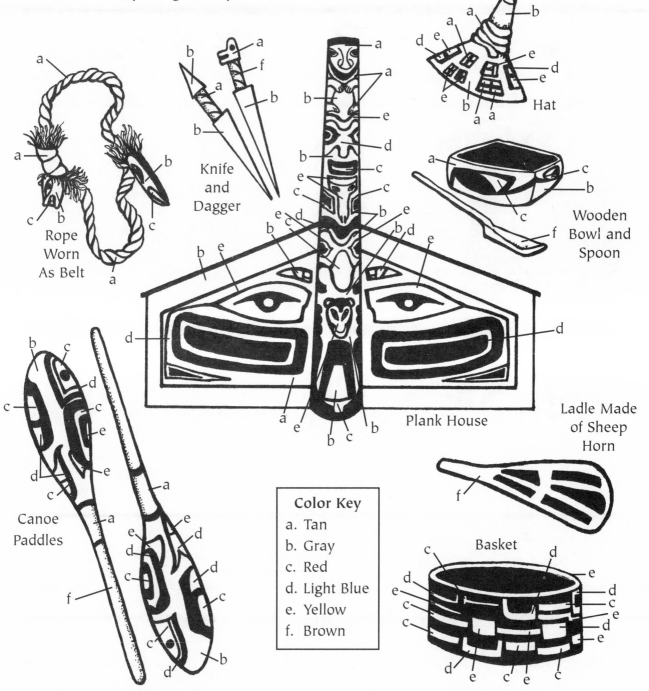

Rope Worn As Belt

Knife and Dagger

Hat

Wooden Bowl and Spoon

Plank House

Ladle Made of Sheep Horn

Canoe Paddles

Color Key
a. Tan
b. Gray
c. Red
d. Light Blue
e. Yellow
f. Brown

Basket

(Teacher's note: Use this page as a flat coloring sheet or enlarge each item to use in one of the special projects described on pages 7-8.)

Native Americans of California

Background Information

Before the arrival of the Spanish about 500 years ago, more than 200,000 Indians lived peacefully together in the place we now call California. It was rare that these Indians went to war. When a member of one tribe did something wrong against another tribe, the punishment was usually a fine of shell money or other trade goods.

How They Survived

Native Americans ate what was available to them within the lands their tribes had lived on for many years. The **Chumash, Costanoan,** and **Salinan** lived along the 2,000-mile coastline. They were expert fishermen who also hunted small animals, dug roots, and gathered wild plants.

Finding food was more difficult for desert tribes like the **Miwok, Washo,** and **Monachi.** They gathered seeds and roots and found interesting ways to use the inner flesh and liquid of cactus plants. These tribes also hunted rabbits, gophers, lizards, grasshoppers, and snakes. The **Shasta, Karok,** and **Yurok,** who lived in the mountain forests, hunted for larger animals like deer and bear.

Deer Hunter

All of the California Indians used acorns as their main food. Acorn flour was used to make hot cereal, bread, and even soup. Before the acorn could be ground into flour, a poison called tanic acid had to be removed. To do this, the women would mix the acorn flour with water and filter it through sand, then grind it once again.

Everyday Customs and Celebrations

An important part of everyday life for California Indians was the sweat house. This small hut was used for meetings, prayers, and to cure certain illnesses. A fire would be built inside the house

FACT

Men of the Pomo tribe were able to carry 100 pounds or more on their backs.

until the room became extremely hot. Men would sit inside until they broke into a sweat. They would then use a thin piece of deer rib to scrape the sweat off their bodies before jumping into a nearby creek. It was believed that the heat could drive away any evil spirit that might make a person ill. Sweating and bathing also helped hide the natural musk, or smell, of a hunter so that the animals he was stalking would not know he was nearby.

California tribes had great feasts for the dead. They believed that if you spoke a dead person's name aloud, he or she would return to Earth. The body, belongings, and dwellings of the dead were burned so their ghosts would not be able to use them.

Many Native Americans living in California tattooed their bodies by pricking their skin with a cactus needle, then rubbing in natural dyes. Men tattooed their chins, arms, and breasts, while women tattooed special designs all over their faces.

The Spanish Bring Change

In 1769 the Franciscan priest Father Junipero Serra and the Spanish army arrived at the place we now call San Diego, where they built the first of 21 missions. The Spanish government wanted to claim the land, and the missionaries, or priests, wanted the Native Americans to become Christians.

Certain tribes, like the **Cahuilla, Diegueno,** and **Serrano,** did adopt European ways. Because so many became Christians and farmers, they were nicknamed Mission Indians. But for other California tribes, living with the Europeans was not easy. Indian men and women were forced to live in separate shelters—even though many were married. They were

Sweat house

made to work long hours in difficult conditions. They were told that their religious beliefs were wrong. This made them feel angry and sad. They wanted to live as they had lived for thousands of years. They wanted to govern, or rule, themselves.

In 1824 the California Indians fought against the Spaniards to win back their lands. Many of the Indians who participated in this fight were killed. Those who tried to run away were caught, chained together, and forced to work even harder for the Spanish. Many died.

Not long afterwards the United States bought much of the West Coast from Mexico. Soon, gold was discovered in northern California. Some miners trespassed on what little land the Indians still claimed, killing entire villages so that they could dig for gold in the streams and rivers. By 1900 only 15,000 Native Americans were still living in California.

Miwok Elderberry
Wood Clapper

How the Dolphin Became Brother to the Chumash
(Chumash)

The earth goddess, Hutash, created the first people out of a magic plant and placed them on Santa Cruz Island. Hutash loved the people and they in turn loved her.

Hutash decided to marry Sky Snake who lives in the part of the sky we call the Milky Way. Sky Snake was so powerful that he could make lightning bolts with his tongue! One day, Sky Snake decided to give the Chumash a gift. He sent a strong lightning bolt down upon the island and started a fire. The people were very grateful because, by keeping the fires burning, they could stay warm and cook their food.

Each year more and more children were born and the villages grew crowded. The noise from the people began to annoy Hutash. She decided that some of the Chumash would have to move off the island and onto the mainland. To help them get to the mainland, Hutash made a rainbow. It stretched from the tallest mountain on Santa Cruz Island to the highest mountains of the mainland coast.

Hutash was very pleased and told her children to move across the rainbow bridge and fill the world with people. As the Chumash began to walk across the bridge, some looked down into the water and fog that swirled below. They became dizzy and fell off the rainbow bridge—down, down, down through the fog and into the ocean.

Hutash felt sorry for her children. After all, she was the one who had told them to cross the bridge in the first place. Hutash did not want her people to drown, so she turned them into dolphins.

This is why all Chumash say that the dolphin is their brother.

Group Project

Petroglyphs on a Sandstone Wall
(Chumash)

The Chumash Indians painted hundreds of symbol pictures, or petroglyphs, on rocks and in caves. It's hard to say what these pictures represent, though some scientists believe they are drawings of dreams and special ceremonies.

Chumash rock painters used natural colors like black, red, and yellow to paint their petroglyphs. They made their brushes from the yucca plant and the wispy ends of animal tails. They used clay pots or shells to hold their paints as they worked.

Before You Begin

- Make enough copies of *For Kids: Petroglyphs* for each of your students. If possible, share one or more of the books on petroglyphs listed in the Bibliography (p.78).

- Point out that petroglyphs are different from the pictograph symbols used by the Plains Indians. While pictographs were strung together like words in a sentence, one petroglyph was probably intended to communicate an entire idea. Encourage students to jot down some of their own ideas about the symbols, then compare different interpretations.

- If possible, take a short nature walk. Brainstorm natural materials you and students could use for paintbrushes. For example, thin and thick twigs could be used for outlining figures, and a cattail might be used for filling in larger spaces.

Materials

- 4 pieces of fine-gauge screen, about 4 x 5 feet (1.2 m x 1.5 m) each OR asphalt roofing shingles
- face mask if using spray glue; thick paintbrush if using diluted glue
- acrylic paints in black, white, bright red, orange, rust, blue, green, and yellow
- paintbrushes or natural materials for applying paints
- newspaper
- sand
- spray glue or diluted white glue
- markers
- white butcher paper
- pushpins
- carbon paper

To Make a Realistic Sandstone "Wall"

(If you are using roofing shingles, skip to step 4.)

1. Lay screens on a flat surface protected with newspaper. (NOTE: if you are using spray glue, complete this step in a well-ventilated area and wear a face mask.) Spray or paint the glue across small sections of the screen, sprinkling sand over each section after it is glued.

2. When glue is completely dry, brush off any excess sand. Most of the sand should stick inside the holes of the screen, producing a rough, yet not overly irregular, surface on which to paint.

3. Maintain your protected work space for later steps.

4. If you are using roofing shingles, use light brown and white tempera paint to spongepaint the surface of each shingle, creating a sandy-looking surface. Let dry before proceeding.

To Design the Petroglyphs

5. Ask students to copy the petroglyph they want to transfer on a piece of white construction paper.

6. Once the designs are completed, ask students to help you decide how to arrange them on screens or roofing shingles. Pin designs in place.

7. Have students slip the carbon paper, dull side up, underneath their designs. They must press hard with a sharp pen or pencil and follow all the lines in order to transfer their drawings to the sandstone wall.

To Finish Designs

8. Remove designs and carbon paper from screens or shingles.

9. Outline each image with bold black paint strokes, then fill in with color.

10. Hang screens around the four walls of your room. Cluster shingles together to create a wall-like effect.

Individual Project
Basket Pottery

The California Indians used baskets and pottery to store food and water so that they could survive during droughts and poor growing seasons. Reeds and grasses were used for baskets; sticky mud and sand were used for pots. Black pitch, or tar, was painted on the insides of pots and baskets to make them waterproof.

Materials (for each student)

- self-drying clay, 1/4 lb
- natural-colored raffia, about 50 grams (available in craft stores)
- water
- white glue
- black acrylic paint
- shellac or hair spray

To Make Coils

1. Pound clay into a round, flat shape, using water to soften the clay as you work.

2. Pinch off some clay and roll it into thin coils, about 1/4–1/2 inch (1.25 cm) thick.

Figure 1

To Make Pottery Base

3. Wind one coil into a small tight circle, 4–5 inches (10–12.5 cm) wide. (Figure 1)

4. Build up the shape by layering moistened coils on top of each other. (Figure 2)

5. Once the coils are in place, smooth out and shape the form.

Figure 2

To Add Basket Weave

6. While pots are still wet, add strands of raffia around the outsides until there is no clay showing. Use fingers or the back of a spoon to push the raffia into the clay so it adheres. (Figure 3)

Figure 3

7. When pot has dried completely (about three days), use black paint to add geometric designs. Paint the insides of pots to mimic pitch.

8. After painted designs are thoroughly dry, protect pots by coating with one layer of shellac or hair spray.

Native Americans of California

Petroglyphs

California Indians chose secret places to record their rock art. They probably did this because each sign was considered very personal to the artist.

Here are some of the symbols they used. What do you think they mean?

65

Native Americans of California

Costumes to Color
(Chumash)

Color the traditional garments by following the key at the bottom of the page.

Color Key
a. Tan
b. Brown
c. Yellow

(Teacher's note: Use this page as a flat coloring sheet or enlarge each item to use in one of the special projects described on pages 7-8.)

Native Americans of California

Tools and Dwellings to Color

Color each item by using the key at the bottom of the page.

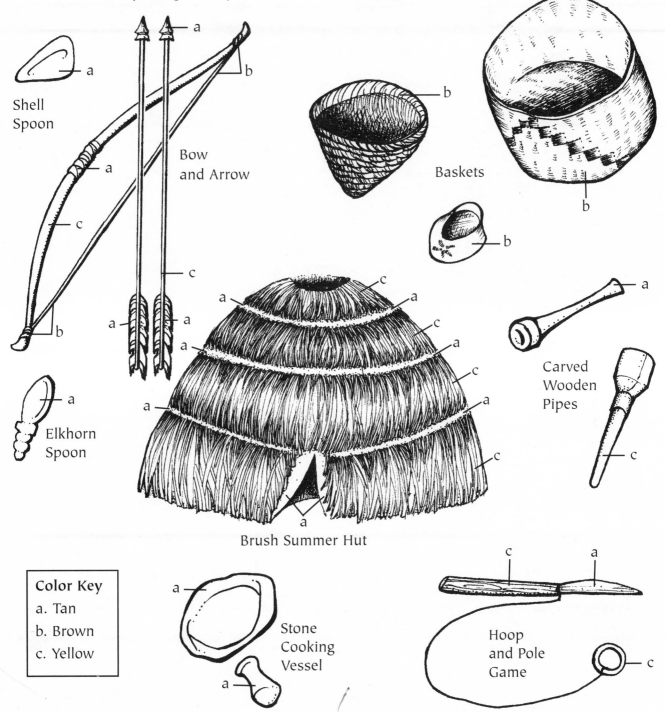

Shell Spoon

Bow and Arrow

Baskets

Elkhorn Spoon

Brush Summer Hut

Carved Wooden Pipes

Color Key
a. Tan
b. Brown
c. Yellow

Stone Cooking Vessel

Hoop and Pole Game

(Teacher's note: Use this page as a flat coloring sheet or enlarge each item to use in one of the special projects described on pages 7-8.)

Native Americans of the Southwest

Zuñi Kachina

Background Information

The Southwest Indians have survived terrible droughts, tribal wars, and European invasions yet have preserved their traditional beliefs more than any other Indian nation.

Southwest groups still live in the land of their ancestors in places we call Colorado, Arizona, New Mexico, Texas, and parts of Mexico. Most of this area is parched, or very dry, desert. Piñon trees and juniper bushes dot the deep canyons and flat plateaus. The lack of flowing water and rain has made living here a challenge over many centuries.

The ancestors of today's Southwest Indians first came to live in the area about 10,000 years ago. These people were nomads who wandered from place to place in search of food.

How They Survived

Scientists call this period of Southwest Indian history the Desert Tradition. The desert people gathered plants that thrived in the harsh climate of scorching hot days and bitter cold nights. They hunted animals such as the woolly mammoth, ground sloth, and even the camel. Eventually, Southwest peoples learned how to grow corn, which became their main food over the next 2,000 years. In fact, corn was so important to the Southwest Indians that they had special ceremonies to honor the growing season.

After these early desert dwellers came their descendants, the Mogollon people. They made permanent settlements by building homes out of clay, wet sand, and wood. The Mogollon people also learned to grow vegetables like squash and beans.

With the invention of farming, the Indians could store food for emergencies. In order to store these extra supplies, the Mogollon people learned to make pottery. They began to decorate their pots with interesting and beautiful designs. Some of the descendants of these people continue the tradition of making beautiful pottery today.

FACT

Ancient Southwest Indians knocked a hole in the center of their pottery so the "spirit" of the vessel could join its owner in the afterlife.

Cities in the Sand

The final group of desert-dwelling Indians were those from the Anasazi Tradition. The Anasazi people developed fortlike cities that could holdas many as 1,000 people. Other Anasazi villages were built inside steep canyon walls. To reach these villages, people had to climb the cliffs by using toeholds carved in rock. Sometimes the Anasazi used long ladders made from the wood of piñon trees to reach their dwellings. When an enemy was approaching, they would quickly lift the ladder up to keep him from entering.

Houses in Anasazi villages were made of wet sand and mud. Inside each house was an underground room called a *kiva*. Kivas were used mainly for religious ceremonies. In the center of the kiva was a deep pit. The Anasazi believed that their ancestors had come up into this world through a hole in the ground. These pits were everyday reminders of their heritage.

The Anasazi people were very inventive. They turned the desert into green farmland by creating dams and reservoirs. They also built over 400 miles of stone roads! The Anasazi region became the main center of trade between Central and North America.

In spite of their success, the Anasazi abandoned their cities and towns in about A.D. 1300. Some people believe that a horrible drought forced these people to find another place to live, but no one is certain.

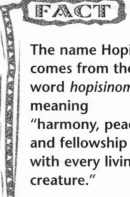

FACT

The name Hopi comes from the word *hopisinom*, meaning "harmony, peace, and fellowship with every living creature."

Other Tribes and Europeans Arrive

Zuñi Fetish

Most of the Native Americans who live in the Southwest today are related to the ancient Anasazi. They are known as the Pueblo Indians. *Pueblo* is a Spanish word meaning "village." The larger Pueblo groups are the **Hopi, Zuñi,** and **Acoma.** Other Native Americans, like the **Navajo** and **Apache,** have lived there for about 600 years.

Spanish explorers and missionaries came to the Southwest from Mexico. They had heard legends of cities with streets paved in gold and silver. They didn't find much gold, but they did find plenty of land that they wanted for themselves.

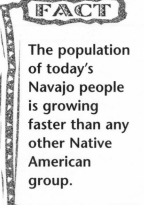

The Spanish people were welcome to live among the Pueblo people at first. They showed the Indians how to grow crops like peaches, melons, and tomatoes as well as how to use iron tools for farming. They also introduced tamed horses, cattle, and sheep to their new friends. But soon the Spanish were demanding more food and materials than the Indians could provide. When the Pueblos could no longer give them the supplies, the Europeans stole what little the Pueblos had left.

Hopi–Wooden Lightening Stick Carried in Dance

The Spanish were also determined to convert the Indians to Christianity. They tried to prevent the Pueblos from practicing their sacred rituals, or kachinas. They tried to tell the Indians what they should believe in. In 1680 the Indians fought against the Spanish, and many were killed.

The arrival of the Spanish did not cause as many problems for the Navajo and Apache Indians. Learning how to raise Spanish cows and horses introduced them to a new way of making a living. They no longer had to depend upon the ups and downs of farming life. Using Spanish horses enabled the Navajo and Apache to trade with Indians from other regions.

Later, when other white settlers arrived in the region, the Navajo and Apache found themselves pushed off their lands. Many now live on reservations in the region.

Navajo Hogan

How Bees Learned to Fly and Peaches Became Sweet (Hopi)

One day Bird Woman went to visit Bee Woman. They spent the day talking about their children, gardens, and other important things. Night came and Bird Woman prepared to leave, but not before she invited Bee Woman to visit her the next day.

In the morning, Bee Woman left very early to go to Bird Woman's home. (This was before bees had wings, so it took them longer to travel anywhere.) Bird Woman lived in an opening of a rock, making it particularly difficult for the little bee to reach her friend. When she finally did, Bird Woman had her sit down and offered some peaches for refreshment.

"I love peaches," Bee Woman replied. "I eat them all the time. However, my friend, these peaches taste a little sour. Would you mind if I made some medicine to make them taste better?"

"That sounds fine," The bird replied. "I look forward to tasting your medicine."

Bee Woman put her honey over the fruit, which now tasted sweeter than ever. In fact, Bird Woman was so thrilled with the results that she said, "You have made my peaches so delicious that I want to do something for you." Then, she pulled out a few of her feathers and made a small pair of wings.

"Now you can fly!" she exclaimed.

But Bee Woman was worried. "I don't know how to fly," she pointed out. Bird Woman understood and showed the bee how it was done.

And ever since that time, peaches have been sweet and bees have flown.

Group Project
Kachina Masks
(Hopi)

Kachinas are believed to be messengers who take the people's prayers to the great forces of nature. They also grant abundant rainfall, children, and everything needed for a good life.

The kachinas represent the spirits of the earth, universe, and sometimes ancient ancestors. It is believed that the person who wears the kachina mask must have a pure heart, for the spirit of a god lives inside the mask.

Before You Start

As a class, examine the *For Kids: Kachina Masks* page. Discuss the different facial elements of each mask. For instance, what features of the Tawa (sun god) mask communicate the properties of the sun? How does the design of the snow god mask make us think of ice crystals? Can students point out the bearlike aspects of the bear kachina?

Materials

– white posterboard in the following sizes:
– 29 x 14 inches (70 cm x 35 cm) (mask base)
– 11 x 6 inches (27.5 x 15 cm) (nose)
– 6 x 6 1/2 inches (15 cm x 16 cm) 2 pieces (ears)
– stapler
– masking tape
– scissors
– tempera paints: yellow, white, black, light blue, green, red
– paintbrushes

To Make a Nose

1. Cut a hole 3 inches (7.5 cm) in diameter in the center of the mask base.

2. Make about five 3-inch (7.5 cm) flaps along one side of the 11 x 6-inch (27.5 x 15 cm) posterboard. (Figure 1)

Figure 1

3. Roll the nose into a cylinder and insert the slit end into the hole of the mask base.

4. Fold down the flaps inside the mask and secure with tape. (Figure 2)

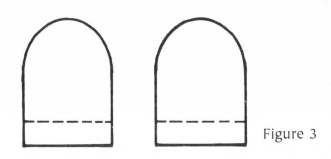

Figure 2

To Make Ears

5. Round the edges on one side of each piece of 6 x 6 1/2-inch (15 cm x 16 cm) posterboard. Fold a 1-inch (2.5 cm) tab on the opposite edges of the posterboard. (Figure 3)

Figure 3

6. Cut one slit on either side of the mask base.

7. Insert an "ear" into each slit so that the tabs are inside. Secure with tape. (Figure 4)

To Finish

8. Roll the mask into a cylinder shape. Slip on the mask and ask a partner to mark the spot where eye slits will be cut. (Children may need help cutting the slits.)

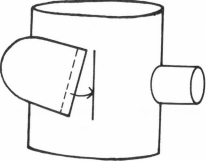

Figure 4

9. Paint according to the chosen mask design.

10. When mask is dry, roll into a cylinder and secure the edges with tape.

Individual Project

Kachina Spirit Doll

The Powamu Ceremony

During this 16-day ceremony, beans are forced to grow quickly in a kiva hothouse. Powamu kachina dancers bless the beans while they are still in the kiva. It is believed that if the beans grow tall, the next summer harvest will be productive.

After blessing the beans, the Powamu dancers distribute bean seeds around the village. Children receive gifts such as bows and arrows and moccasins. The ugly Soyoko kachinas appear to children who have been naughty throughout the year. The kachinas pretend they will take children from their parents if the children do not change their behavior. Parents beg for their children and pay a food ransom to Soyoko.

After the ceremony, children are given a kachina doll carved from the roots of a cottonwood tree.

Materials

– 11-inch (27.5 cm) wooden closet rod OR cardboard paper towel roll
– tempera paints: white, black, green, red, and yellow
– paintbrushes
– feathers
– leather strips
– beads

To Make the Doll

1. Paint the rod white. Let dry.

2. Sketch the desired kachina face onto the rod. Trace lines with black marker.

3. Embellish the rod with Hopi designs and symbols. Paint.

4. Add feathers, fake fur, leather strips, beads, and other decorative items.

5. Ask students to work cooperatively to write puppet shows or stage scripts based on the Powamu Ceremony.

Native Americans of the Southwest

Kachina Masks

Kachina masks use colors to show from which direction each god came: North, South, East, or West. Here are some of the masks and directions for coloring them.

Qoqlo, a birdlike god

face—black
decorations—white

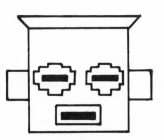

Snow kachina

face—blue
eyes—white

Dragonfly kachina

face—black
stripes—red

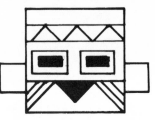

Making Thunder kachina

face—green
forehead squares—
red and yellow

Bear kachina

face, left side—dark yellow
face, right side—green

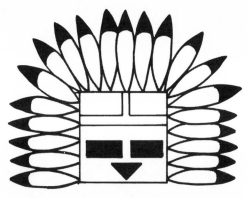

Tawa, the sun god

forehead—one yellow rectangle, one red rectangle
face—green
feathers—white with black tips

Ogre

face—black
forehead marks—green
cheeks, teeth—white

Soyoko

face—black

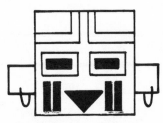

Ongchoma, the compassionate kachina

face—green
eyes—purple and black
cheek marks—black

For Kids

Native Americans of the Southwest

**Costumes to Color
(Hopi)**

Color the traditional garments by following the key below.

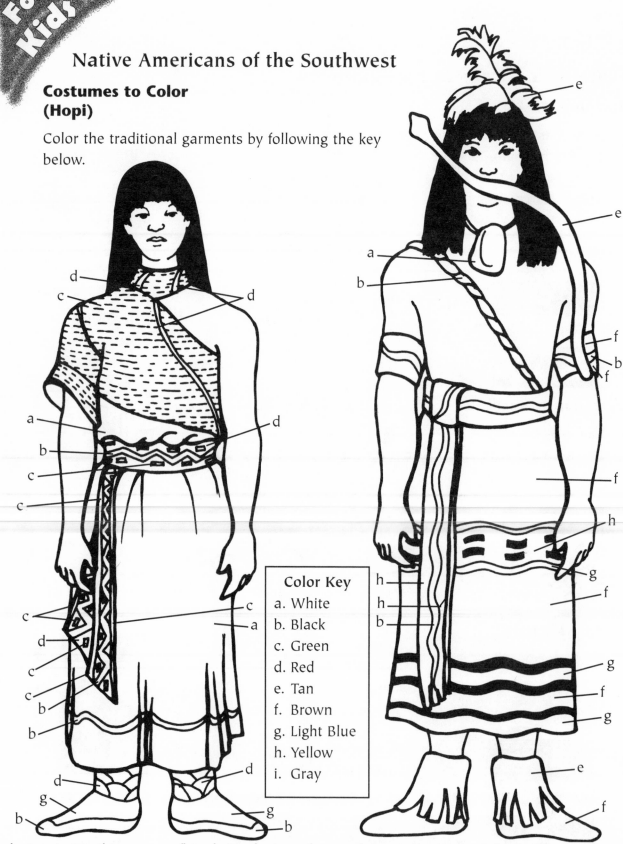

Color Key
a. White
b. Black
c. Green
d. Red
e. Tan
f. Brown
g. Light Blue
h. Yellow
i. Gray

(Teacher's note: Use this page as a flat coloring sheet or enlarge each item to use in one of the special projects described on pages 7-8.)

Native Americans of the Southwest

Tools and Dwellings to Color

Color each item by using the color key below.

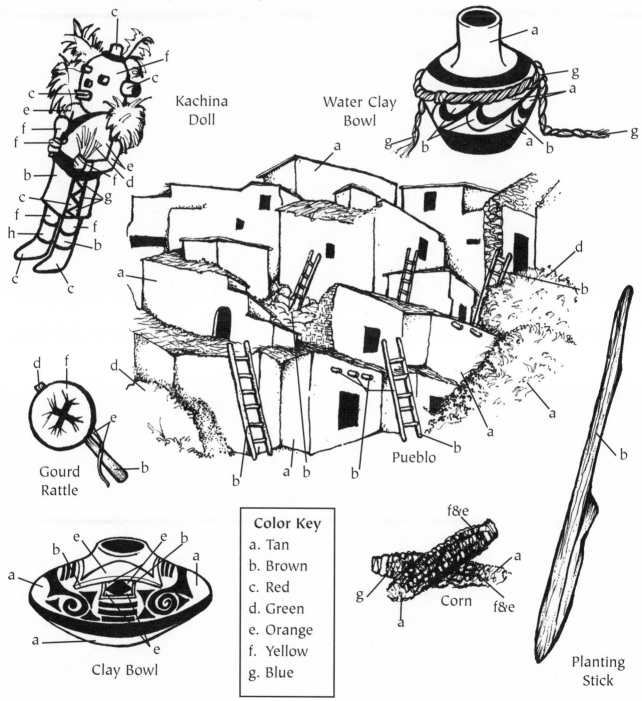

Kachina Doll

Water Clay Bowl

Gourd Rattle

Pueblo

Clay Bowl

Corn

Planting Stick

Color Key
a. Tan
b. Brown
c. Red
d. Green
e. Orange
f. Yellow
g. Blue

(Teacher's note: Use this page as a flat coloring sheet or enlarge each item to use in one of the special projects described on pages 7-8.)

Bibliography

General Reference Books

After Columbus: The Smithsonian Chronicles of the North American Indians by Herman J. Viola (Smithsonian Books, 1990).

Keepers of the Night: Native American Stories and Nocturnal Activities for Children; Keepers of the Earth: Native American Stories and Environmental Activities for Children; Keepers of the Animals: Native American Stories and Wildlife Activities for Children by Michael Caduto and Joseph Bruchac (Fulcrum, 1988, 1991, 1994).

A History of US: The First Americans by Joy Hakim (Oxford, 1993).

Myths of the North American Indians by Lewis Spence (Gramercy Books, 1994).

Children's Literature

A Boy Becomes a Man at Wounded Knee by Ted Wood with Wanbli Numpa Afraid of Hawk (Walker, 1992).

Around the World in a Hundred Years: From Henry the Navigator to Magellan by Jean Fritz (Putnam, 1994).

The Cahuilla by John Bean Lowell and Lisa Bourgeault (Chelsea House, 1992).

California Missions: The Earliest Views Made in 1856 (The Journals and Drawings of Henry Miller) (Bellerphon Books, 1995).

California's Indians and the Gold Rush by Clifford E. Trafzer (Sierra Oaks Publishing, 1989).

Children of Clay: A Family of Pueblo Potters by Rina Swentzell (Lerner, 1992).

The Chippewa by Jacqueline D. Green (Franklin Watts, 1993).

Dancing Teepees: Poems of American Indian Youth selected by Virginia Driving Hawk Sneve (Holiday House, 1989).

Dragonfly's Tale by Kristina Rodanas (Clarion, 1991).

Eagle Drum on the Powwow Trail: With a Young Grass Dancer by Robert Crum (Four Winds Press, 1994).

The First Thanksgiving by Jean Craighead George (Philomel, 1993).

Houses of Bark by Bonnie Shemie (Tundra Books, 1990).

Indian Signals and Sign Language by George Fronval and Daniel Dubois (Wings Books, 1994).

An Indian Winter by Russell Freedman (Holiday House, 1992).

The Iroquois by Barbara Graymont (Chelsea House, 1988).

The Iroquois by Dean R. Snow (Blackwell Publishing, 1994).

Ishi: The Last of His Tribe by Theodora Kroeber (Bantam Books, 1989).

The Micmac: How Their Ancestors Lived 500 Years Ago by Ruth Holmes Whitehead and Harder McGee (Nimbers Publishing, 1985).

Monster Slayer by Vee Browne (Northland, 1991).

Navajo: Visions and Voices from Across the Mesa (poems) by Shonto Begay (Scholastic, 1995).

The Ojibwa by Helen Hornbeck Tanner (Chelsea House, 1992).

Pueblo Boy: Growing Up in Two Worlds by Marcia Keegan (Cobblehill/Dutton, 1991).

A River Ran Wild by Lynne Cherry (Harcourt, Brace, Jovanovich, 1992).

The Sad Night: The Story of an Aztec Victory and a Spanish Loss by Sally Schofer Mathews (Clarion, 1994).

The Sioux by Elaine Landau (Franklin Watts, 1991).

Totem Pole by Diane Hoyt-Goldsmith (Holiday House, 1990).

When Jaguars Ate the Moon and Other Stories About Animals and Plants of the Americas by Maria Cristina Brusca and Tona Wilson (Henry Holt, 1995).

Software

500 Nations CD-ROM (Microsoft Corporation, Redmond, Wash.). A comprehensive guide to Native American history in which students can tour historic structures, listen to Indian music, and examine art up close.

Additional Books

Native Americans of the Far North

Rock Art of the North American Indian by Campbell Grant (Cambridge University Press, 1983).

The American Indians Series: People of the Lakes (Time-Life Books, 1994).

Native Americans of the Northeast Woodlands

Nagwenta-lay-ay-ha: Traditional Faceless Cornhusk Doll (American Indian Education Commission, 1986).

Native Americans of the Southeast

The American Indians Series: Tribes of the Southern Woodlands (Time-Life Books, 1994).

The Cherokees by Eileen Lucas. (Millbrook Press, 1993).

Then & Now Series: Indians of the Southeast by Burt, Jesse, and Robert B. Ferguson (Abingdon Press, 1973).

Native Americans of the Northwest Coast

Symbolic Immortality: The Tlingit Potlatch of the Nineteenth Century by Sergei Kan (Smithsonian Institute Press, 1989).

Totem Pole by Diane Hoyt-Goldsmith (Holiday House, 1990).

Myths and Legends of the Haida of the Northwest by Martine J. Reid, Ph.D. (Bellerphon Books, 1995).

Northwest Coast: Essays and Images From the Columbia River to the Cook Inlet by Bradford Matson (Thunder Bay Press, 1991).

Native Americans of the Great Plains

From the Heart of the Crow Country: The Crow Indians' Own Stories by Joseph Medicine Crow (Orion Books, 1992).

The Plains Indians: Their Origins, Migrations and Cultural Development by Francis Haines (Thomas Y. Crowell, 1976).

The First People by Jack-Standing Elk Howlett (Pamphlet). American Indian Education Commission, Los Angeles, CA.

Native Americans of California

California Indians (Pamphlet) American Indian Education Commission, Los Angeles, CA.

The Chumash by Jill Duvall (Children's Press, 1994).

California Indians: An Illustrated Guide by George Emanuels (Diablo Books, 1991).

The First American Series: California Indians by C.L. Keyworth (Facts On File, 1991).

California's Chumash Indians: A Project of the Santa Barbara Museum of Natural History Educational Center (EZ Nature Books, 1990).

A Field Guide to Rock Art symbols of the Greater Southwest by Alex Patterson (Johnson Books, 1992).

Native Americans of the Southwest

Southwestern Indian Arts and Crafts by Mark Bahti (K.C. Publications, 1992).

Ancient Pueblo Peoples by Linda Cordell (St. Remy Press and Smithsonian Institute, 1994).

Southwest Indians: A Photographic Journey by Bill Harris (Crescent Books, 1993).

Miniatures of the Southwest by Nancy Schiffer (Schiffer Publications, 1991).

The Hopi Indians by Bryan P. Sears (Chelsea House Publishers, 1994).